YOGODA

OR

TISSUE-WILL SYSTEM OF PHYSICAL PERFECTION

By
SWAMI YOGANANDA, B.A
OF INDIA

PUBLISHED BY
SAT-SANGA
3O HUNTINGTON AVENUE
BOSTON, MASS.

Editing of this 2013 reprint is by Donald Castellano-Hoyt, San Antonio, Texas. He has just published his first book on religious and spiritual topics, *The Eternal Religion: Glimpses of Divine Glory*, CreateSpace Independent Printers, available now at local book stores and CreateSpace, https://www.createspace.com/4506928. Donald may be reached at **dcastellano.hoyt@gmail.com**.

EVERETT PRINTING SERVICE

Table of Contents

INTRODUCTION

1. Will is the great dynamo lying within us. The direction of Will is the fundamental principle of **YOGODA**. The more you apply Will, when asked to do so in the following exercises, the better results you will get. Never forget this. If you neglect this while taking the exercises, you will miss the thing of chief importance.

    Remember, whenever you direct your Will into any part of the body as you tense it you are sending down a quantity of nerve energy - - Pranic current or vital energy - - from the brain to that part. The greater the flow of this Pranic current, the stronger and better is its action on that particular part, and the greater is the chance of the tissues of that part being revitalized by more rapid circulation and healthier Pranic adjustment. Thus tissues will grow stronger and fresher. In the tension of muscles by Will you turn on the Pranic current in them, in relaxation you switch it off. This Pranic current (or motor nerve energy) sent down by Will is not only an independent source of power to the muscles and others parts but it is also a most active agent in bringing about a better adjustment of the tissues. It imparts more life to them, too. So remember, while inducing high tension in a muscle or group of muscles, to use *maximum Will*.

    This is conscious Will as differentiated from automatic will, such as is used in walking, etc. But when you walk blind-folded in the dark you have to use conscious Will, and then you necessarily send down more nerve energy to the muscles and touch-surfaces for better limb movement.

    * * * * * *

    An automobile battery needs to be recharged once in a while when run down. So the battery of the body parts, exhausted by physical work and brain labor, requires to be recharged by fresh nerve current sent down by Will. You will immediately get over fatigue by performing **YOGODA** exercises. You will also feel wonderful freshness, and your muscles will become more and more powerful.

2.   After you have once formed an idea of the whole system, it will not require more than 15 minutes to perform all the important exercises of YOGODA, except of course the Technique of Concentration. **[Original Pamphlet p. 1]**

3.   In case of indigestion or constipation or similar troubles the abdominal exercises are to be done at least 15 times (20 or more, if needed). This will require a little more time. The exercises should be done either early in the morning or four hours after a heavy meal. When rightly done, they will cause better peristaltic action of the intestines and more uniform secretion of the glands — liver, pancreas, etc. If constipation bothers you, the bowels will move within one hour after the exercises.

4.   YOGODA exercises can be taken in the morning, or at any time when the stomach is not much loaded.

5.   Exercises marked ✪ must be taken daily.
Those that are not so marked may be taken two or three days apart, as convenient.

6.   Perform the general tension exercise and relaxation in bed, as soon as you wake up. Don't jump from your bed without adjusting the whole body.

7.   For specific cases of bodily ailments or for adjustment of special bodily parts the number of times for particular exercises is to be increased, when so instructed.

8.   Slow and attentive exercises performed once produces more beneficial results than hasty and inattentive exercise performed many times.

9.   YOGODA EXERCISES are always to be begun with this

AFFIRMATION

O Eternal Energy! awaken within me conscious will, conscious vitality, conscious health; goodwill to all, vitality in all, good health to all.

O Eternal Energy! I am a tenant in the body, sent here by Thy grace to rule the body but never to be ruled by it.

O Eternal Energy! by Thy power I know that in tension I put forth energy into the body and in relaxation I withdraw it. Youth of body and mind abide in me forever, forever, forever.

> *My mind! awake, sleep no more;*
> *Awake, sleep no more;*
> *Awake, sleep no more.*
> *Peace! Peace! Peace!*

10. Before taking YOGODA exercises air the room as thoroughly as you can. In winter close the windows before beginning.

11. REMINDER: Never forget that when you are tensing particular parts with Will you are sending down fresh Life Energy from the brain to those parts and body cells – that you are recharging the body battery from the motor centers **[Original Pamphlet p. 2]** of the brain. Always feel this while taking YOGODA. Through the power of Will the brain receives an increased supply of Life Energy from Cosmic Energy residing in and surrounding the body, through certain parts—pineal gland, medulla oblongata, etc. Sleep recharges the body battery *automatically* and *partially*. YOGODA does that *consciously, actively, and much more fully*. CONCENTRATION LESSONS (see them) do that conscious-super-consciously, *silently, and completely*.

12. For reducing fat, perform especially the following exercises a greater number of times than mentioned in the lessons: Figs. **5, 26, 28, 29, 37, 38, 39, 40**. Do not exercise too much in one day. Increase gradually. EAT LESS STARCH FOR A WHILE, NO CANDIES, NO CREAM, NO PASTRY, AND LESS WATER. Keep slightly hungry after each meal. Also do exercise D (Fig. 37, *a, b*) as many times as possible without consideration of tension or breathing.

13. VERY IMPORTANT: While taking the YOGODA exercises connected with breathing, viz., Figs. **2**, **3**, **26**, **36**, **37 (a, b)** [*sic*], and spinal exercise (a), inhale and exhale SLOWLY, and with ease TO THE FULL EXTENT, without putting too much effort on the chest and diaphragm, and make a kind of suppressed (though distinctly audible and rounded) guttural sound "aw," while inhaling, and "ee" while exhaling (mouth closed all the time). With the head almost erect and pressing the underside of the chin slightly against throat (not against the chest), those sounds can easily be made. Putting more attention on the making of these sounds with the help of the breath than on the bare act of breathing in or out helps gradual and slow intake of breath while inhaling and gradual and slow release of it while exhaling. There shouldn't be much heaving of the chest. Never breathe in or out quickly or jerkily. Inhalation and exhalation should take the same length of time (maximum, 30 seconds for each, to be attained gradually). By a little practice you will get the breathing all right.

14. Take a fresh air walk daily for at least two miles.

15. Try, as much as possible, to do without white bread and foods made of white flour. Use graham, brown, whole-wheat, vitamin [sic], or rye bread. Do not eat too much meat. Not more than a cup of tea or coffee daily, if at all. Two glasses of milk at least.

16. Practice moderation in all the activities of your daily life.

17. While not neglecting the other exercises, especial attention is to be devoted to the following: Figs. **2**, **3**, **26**, **29**, **31**, **36**, **37**, together with the Spinal exercises and the Abdominal exercises. Increase to the maximum number of times in as few days as possible. If you get tired or your head seems to feel **[Original Pamphlet p. 3]** fagged after work, immediately do Fig. 36 several times in the fresh air or near open window (not, of course in a draft). Besides the above, all other exercises marked ✪ it is very important to do regularly, gradually increasing the number of times.

18. It is slow but sure suicide to walk, sit, rest, talk, sit at table, or lie with a caved-in chest. The lung cells are starved thereby, and mal-adjustments of the vertebrae occur. So it is absolutely

necessary always to have the chest forward and shoulder blades a little backward, even when leaning back against a chair for rest. Practice will relieve irksomeness.

19. SECOND REMINDER: The *more slowly* the exercises are done, *with deliberate application of the Will Power* to the particular parts, the greater is the flow of Lite Energy from the brain to those parts, and the more harmonious its co-ordination with the cellular energy of the tissues. There is also more squeezing of the waste materials out of the tissues, this waste being finally expelled through the nostrils, pores, etc. Both greater oxygenation, caused by deep breathing, and fuller circulation, due to the tension of particular parts, are reinforced by the distribution of motor Life Energy to the different parts through Will Power. *This complete coordination* gives health, power, freshness and long life. By this process you store up more cellular energy than you USE UP DURING daily activities.

Though the forms of some of the exercises later described may be commonly known, the simultaneous coordination of breathing, muscular tension, and direction of Life Energy through Will, as advised in each exercise, constitutes the uniqueness of YOGODA.

20. While tensing and otherwise exercising body parts, and sending into them Life Energy through conscious Willing, never forget to awaken in yourself the deep reverential consciousness that you are trying to contact the Omnipotent Cosmic Spiritual Energy, as vitalizing your body. It is another point which differentiates YOGODA from purely mechanical methods. The progress of the student will be in the degree that he recognizes and applies the above truths.

ADOMINAL EXERCISES
✪✪ ADOMINAL EXERCISES

These are special exercises for those who particularly want to improve digestion and eliminate constipation and other abdominal troubles by increasing the peristaltic movements of the intestines and the secretions of the glands — liver, pancreas, etc.—in a proper way. Those without any abdominal troubles may equally well take them without any harm.

They are indispensably necessary for all.

(a) See **Fig. 27**.

(b) Perform on an empty stomach the exercise in **Fig. 28** from **[Original Pamphlet p. 4]** 15 to 40 times, not, of course, the first day. Increase the number of times daily by 5, 6, or more, till you reach the maximum number, without feeling sore in the upper abdominal muscles. Morning or evening,

(c) While continuing (a) and (b) try to do the footnote exercise of **Fig. 28** in this way: Taking the same position and with breath expelled, try on REAL empty stomach to bulge out with a little force the vertical muscles of the abdomen (not the whole abdomen) in the form of a vertical tube, and then let them down. Alternately, from 10 to 25 (maximum) times, to be increased gradually every day. Do this for at least 15 days.

(d) When you think you can do (c), then, taking the some position and having breath expelled, try on REAL empty stomach, with the contributory rotating movement of the hips from left to right, to make the vertical, tube-like muscles play in vertical waves on the abdomen from left to right. After several weeks' practice dispense with the movement of the hips, and then, by remaining still and bending over and exhaling the breath, try to produce those waves. With practice you will get it right. Ten to thirty times, to be gradually increased. When you are able to do this exercise properly, you need not do (a), (b), and (c). Until then continue (a), (b), and (c), along with (d).

Its effect is simply marvelous. It is worth many times the time and effort you put into it. You will get substantial results, even with (a), (b) and (c).

SPINAL EXERCISES

✪✪SPINAL EXERCISES

(a) Bending the left leg at the knee, sit on the left heal and foot and stretch the right leg on the floor. Inhale fully.

Now with your chin firmly placed on your chest try to bring your forehead in touch with the cap of the right knee while both hands grasp the toes of the right foot. Hold the breath, mentally counting 1 to 6, and keep your forehead down as near the right kneecap as possible. (Daily try to make your forehead go down and down until it can be kept in touch with the kneecap of the straightened leg on the floor for a longer and longer time. Maximum mental counting, 1 to 12, to be increased gradually.) Then exhale. Next do the exercise stretching the left leg on the floor and folding the right leg. Then stretching both legs on the floor, burying head between the knees. Do the entire exercise daily at least four times, more by and by (maximum, 8 times). This is the greatest method for adjusting the entire spinal vertebrae and pads. It relieves undue pressure on the nerves issuing from between the vertebrae (the cause of so many diseases), brings freshness, and prevents colds and innumerable ailments.

(b) Stand erect, with feet apart. Stretch both arms in front. Now with a little force swing your arms, body, and face 'way [sic] to the left and back and then 'way [sic] to the right and back, alternately, 3 times. Do this exercise gently, at least for the first week. You will hear the crack of the vertebrae.
(c) See **Fig. 31.**
[Original Pamphlet p. 5]

Figure 1

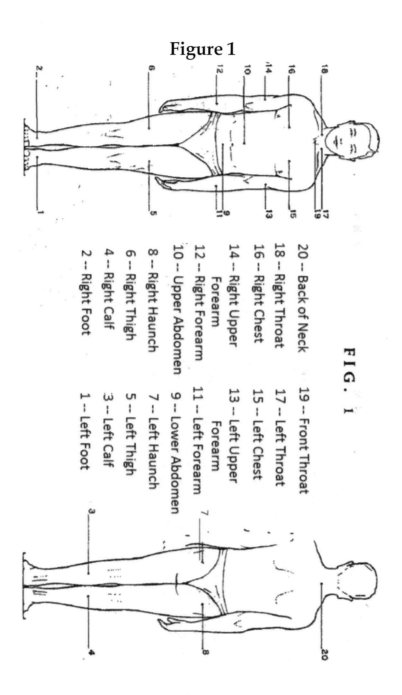

FIG. 1

20 -- Back of Neck   19 -- Front Throat
18 -- Right Throat   17 -- Left Throat
16 -- Right Chest   15 -- Left Chest
14 -- Right Upper   13 -- Left Upper
        Forearm   Forearm
12 -- Right Forearm   11 -- Left Forearm
10 -- Upper Abdomen   9 -- Lower Abdomen
8 -- Right Haunch   7 -- Left Haunch
6 -- Right Thigh   5 -- Left Thigh
4 -- Right Calf   3 -- Left Calf
2 -- Right Foot   1 -- Left Foot

LESSON ONE -- PART I

Enumeration of Twenty Body Parts to be Exercised

First memorize the list of body parts from the chart. The muscles have been separated into twenty groups as the divisions of the body fall between the principal articulations — ankles, knees, hips, waist, elbows, shoulders, and neck. See **Fig. 1.**

Memorize the number of body parts (odd numbers left, even numbers right) of **Fig. 1.**

Position

1. Stand with center of gravity in the middle of the feet.
2. Lift chest.
3. Erect the spinal column (be careful not to bend the body forward or backward, right or left).
    To secure the above position, do the following: Extend the arms, making a perfect cross with the spinal column.
    Holding strongly at the center of the cross, drop arms at sides, retaining the central position.

Poise

Then poise by carrying weight of the body forward, chest leading;
Then bunk to center of feet again;
Then back to the heels, still with forward chest;
Then to center again;
Then rise on toes several times.

Relaxation

1. Hold the spinal column erect.
2. Close eyes.
3. Relax the body parts (general relaxation).
4. Relax the twenty body parts in order, from *1 to 20*, centering consciousness successively in each part (specific relaxation).
5. Slightly vibrate and relax, *1 to 20 parts*, to ensure freedom.
6. Move the shoulders twice swinging arms loosely.
7. Be still and feel that you are withdrawing all strength along with your Nerve Energy to the spine and brain, and that your limbs are limp and powerless.
8. Hold relaxation one or two minutes, eyes closed all the time.
    Relaxation may also be practiced while lying down.
    Stretch and elongate the body and relax as above.

[Original Pamphlet p. 6]

LESSON ONE --PART II

"Tense with Will; Relax and feel" *

Key

Mechanical and Will Movements of Muscles Compared

Example (A)

1. Extend right arm in front.
2. Place left hand on right biceps.
3. Bend right arm at elbow, observing the automatic contraction of biceps through the *mechanical movement.*

Note that the action of the Will is in the bending of the arm and not in the contraction of the biceps.

Example (B)

1. Relax right arm loosely at side.
2. With left hand grasp lightly the biceps of the right arm.
3. Close eyes.
4. Then without bending right arm at elbow *tense the biceps* slowly to the maximum of force *with WILL.*
5. Sense the tensing.
6. Permit no mechanical movement of the arm.
7. Then relax slowly.

Note that this tensing of biceps, if done successfully by the novice, is the *direct action of the Will on the muscle.* If the novice is not successful with the upper arm, let him make the experiment with the forearm, which may he easier with some.

Preliminary Practices■

 (1). Note three degrees of tension (or stiffening):

Tense Low: Grasp the right forearm with the left hand. Close fist. Slightly energize the right forearm to get Low Tension. Hold two seconds.

Tense Medium: Then energize it a little more to get Medium *Tension.* Hold two seconds.

Tense High: Then use maximum energy to get High Tension. Hold two seconds. Relax.

---

*Remember   this   motto   all   through   the   exercises.
■-- 1. This principle is the key to the exercise of all body parts. -- 2. Begin tensing each time by centralizing consciousness in the middle of each   part.   --   3.   Completely   relax   each   time   before   tensing. REMEMBER THESE.

[Original Pamphlet p. 7]

These three forms of tension may be practiced in other body parts.

(2) Partial Relaxation

Induce high tension in right forearm with closed fist.
Then partially relax.
Hold, counting 1 to 5.

(3) Complete Relaxation

1. Then relax completely.
   Repeat three times.

****

MAIN EXERCISE

✪ ✪ See **Figs. 2 and 3** *

1. Stand erect.
2. Eyes level.
3. Relax.

■ 4. *Inhale gradually* to the full extent, then, with Will sent to all body parts simultaneously, quickly TENSE ■■ THEM HIGH *at once* (don't tense the throat muscles), jumping wide, closing fists, and pressing arms against sides.

5. Hold tension and breath, mentally counting 1 to 5.

■■ 6. Exhale *gradually* and relax all body parts.

7. Draw right foot up to left.

Repeat at least three times, more by and by. Maximum, 5 times.

*Follow the instructions minutely. A little negligence will hinder attainment   of   the   best   results.
■ See **Instruction 13, Page 3**. [current document P. 7 and above]
■■ See **Instructions 1, 11, 19**, and **Page 1** [current document P. 5 and above], **Page 2** [current document P. 6 and above], **and Page 4.** [current document P. 9 and above]
[Original Pamphlet p. 8]

FIGURES 2, 3, AND 4

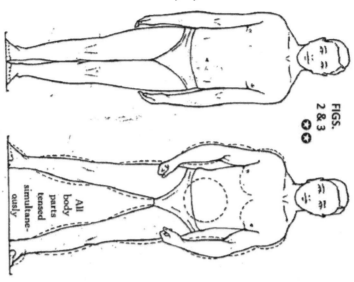

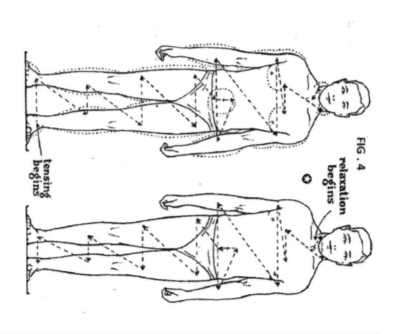

LESSON ONE — PART III

"Tense with will; Relax and feel."*

⭐ EXERCISE (A). **See Fig. 4**

1. Stand erect.
2. Close eyes.
3. Relax body parts 1 to 20 (down up.). ■
4. Hold relaxation half a minute without moving.
5. Place attention on center of instep of left foot.
6. Slowly tense high, drawing the toes up.
7. Keep it tensed. ■■
8. Go on adding tension with Will in the same manner, in all 20 body parts, "down up" successively.
9. Hold all 20 parts tensed, breath held, mentally counting 1 to 6, and quickly noting mentally whether all parts are tensed or not.
10. Exhale and slowly relax the chain of tensed parts "Up down," in inverse order, from 20 to 1. If, while relaxing the parts above the waist, you find that you have also unintentionally relaxed the parts below the waist, then simultaneously tense again all the parts below the waist and relax from waist down one by one.
Repeat thrice.

⭐ EXERCISE (B). **See Fig. 5**

1. Stand erect and firm.
2. Straighten right arm in front, palm downward.
3. Clench fist.
4. Rotate over in largest possible circles from front to back with a free swing, loudly counting 1 to 4, 4 times, each time humming 1-2-3-4 in one sustained breath.

Repeat same with left arm, then with both arms together, striking palms in front.

*Remember this all through the exercises.
■ Ladder of *Paris*.
"Down up" means attention passing through the centre of each part from left to right alternately upward, 1 to 20.
"Up down" means attention passing through the centre of each part in inverse order, from 20 to 1.
■■While tensing one part by WILL disregard the slight tension, in the beginning, if any, of the adjoining parts. Practice will gradually make these parts operate separately. More attention to the part exercised and less to others will bring about this result.

[Original Pamphlet p. 9]

FIGURES 5-7 AND 8-11

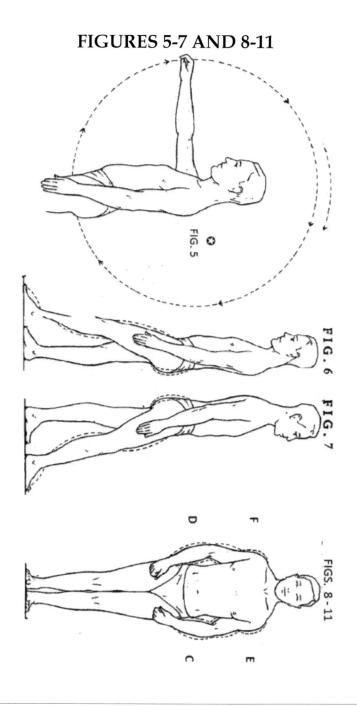

LESSON TWO-PART 1 *

"Tense with will; Relax and feel." ■

EXERCISE (A). **Fig. 6**

Stand erect.

Relax

Close eyes.

Put weight of body on right foot.

Extend left foot diagonally forward.

Slowly tense left foot high, drawing the toes up.

Relax.

Tense high again.

Relax.

Repeat exercise thrice or more. Repeat exercise in left calf, thigh, and haunch. Put you attention in each part and feel at least the thigh and haunch with your hand to see whether they are being tensed or not.

EXERCISE (B). **Fig. 7**

Put weight on left foot.

Extend right foot diagonally forward.

Repeat preceding exercise with right foot, right calf, right thigh and right haunch. Put your attention there and feel at least the thigh and haunch with your hand to see whether they are being tensed or not. Return to position.

EXERCISE (C). **Fig. 8**

Arms loose at sides.

Center attention in left forearm.

Slowly tense it *High*, closing fist, up to the point when you feel that the left upper arm is about to become automatically tensed.

Relax slowly.

Repeat thrice or more.

EXERCISE (D). **Fig. 9**

Repeat Exercise with Right Forearm.

*While taking these exercises center attention completely on parts exercised, disregarding the slight tension in the beginning, if any, of the adjoining parts. Practice will gradually make these parts operate separately. More attention to the parts exercised and less to others brings about this result. In all these exercises deliberation is more important than umber of repetitions, i.e., *a few times slowly are better than many times fast.*

All these exercises to be taken with closed eyes. ■Remember this motto all through the exercises. Follow the instructions minutely. A little negligence will hinder attainment of the best results.

[Original Pamphlet p. 10]

FIGURES 12, 13, 14 THRU 17

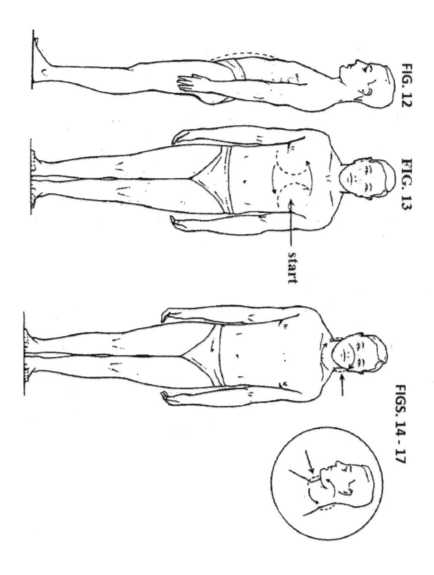

EXERCISE (E). **Fig. 10**

Tense high left upper arm, holding the lower left arm with fingers out-stretched at right angles to it and pressing the upper arm against the side.

Repeat Thrice.

Relax.

EXERCISE (F). **Fig. 11**

Same exercise with right upper arm.

EXERCISE (G). **Fig. 12**

Hold position,

Tense high and relax abdominal muscles alternately, three times or more, centering attention there.

EXERCISE (H). Fig. **13**

Hold erect body position.

Tense high and alternately relax upper chest muscles thrice or more, left and right separately. At the beginning press left arm a little at left side when the left chest muscle is tensed. Do same while tensing right chest muscle.

Exercise (I). **Figs. 14, 15, 16, 17**

Exercise in the same way with:

Left Throat, bending head a little to the left.

Right Throat, bending head a little to the right.

Front Throat, bending head a little forward.

Back of Neck, bending head a little backward.

✪ Exercise (J). **Fig. 18**

Grasp back of chair with right hand keeping weight on right foot.

Lift left foot and swing it in a circle, loudly counting 1 to 4 four times, humming each time 1-2-3-4 in one sustained breath.

Return to position.

✪ Exercise (K). **Fig. 19**

Repeat Exercise (J) with right foot.

✪ Exercise (L). **Fig. 20**

1. Stand erect.
2. Tense muscles of back and neck and scapulas by bending the head backwards and lifting arms slowly from sides to horizontal.
3. Hold neck firm while relaxing arms or sides.

Repeat four times.

[Original Pamphlet p. 11]

FIGURES 18 AND 19

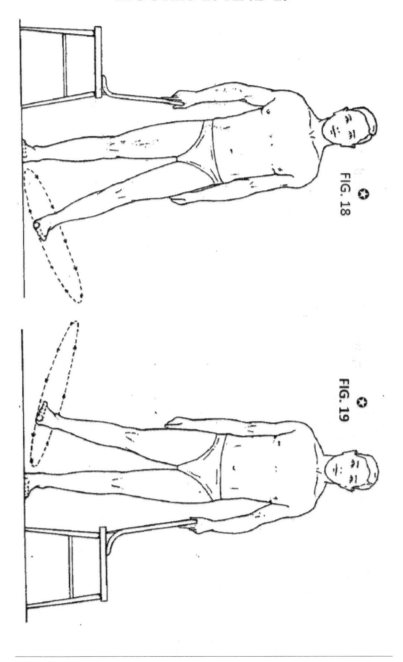

FIG. 18

FIG. 19

LESSON TWO -- PART II *

"Tense with will; Relax and feel." ∎

(A). Cross Tension, **Fig. 21**

    1. Stand erect with feet a little apart.

    2. Relax.

    3. Slowly tense left foot HIGH, drawing the toes up; then relax.

    a. See (*a*) **Fig. 21**.

    4. Immediately follow it up by HIGH tension and relaxation of right foot.

Repeat thrice alternately, left and right.

    Exercise similarly three times, with left and right calf.

    Exercise similarly three times, with left and right thigh.

    Exercise similarly three times, with left and right haunch.

    Exercise similarly three times, with left and right forearm, closing fist.

    Exercise similarly three times, with left and right upper arm (lower arm at right angles to it).

(B). LENGTHWISE TENSION. **Figs. 22, 23**

    1. Stand erect.

    2. Relax.

    3. Extend left foot diagonally forward. See (*a*) **Figs. 22, 23.**

    4. Put weight on right foot.

    5. Left foot tense HIGH.

    6. Relax.

    7. Immediately after tense left calf HIGH – relax.

Alternate thrice.

(*b*) Repeat same exercise with left calf and left thigh, alternating three times (feel tension and relaxation with hand).

(*c*) Then with left thigh and left haunch. While tensing left haunch put weight of body on left leg. Feel tension and relaxation with hand.

Fig. 24

Repeat same series with right foot and right calf three times ALTERNATELY. See (*a*) **Fig. 24**.

Repeat with right calf and right thigh three times alternately. See (*b*) above.

Same with right thigh and right haunch. See (*c*) above.

  *While taking these exercises center attention and Will completely in parts exercised, disregarding the slight tension, in the beginning, if any, of the adjoining parts. Gradually these parts will operate separately. More attention to the part exercised and less to others brings about this result.

  ∎Remember this motto all through the exercises.

[Original Pamphlet p. 12]

FIGURES 20 AND 21

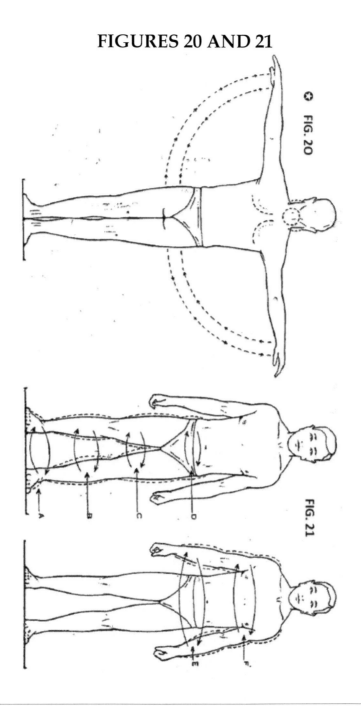

FIGURES 22, 23, AND 24

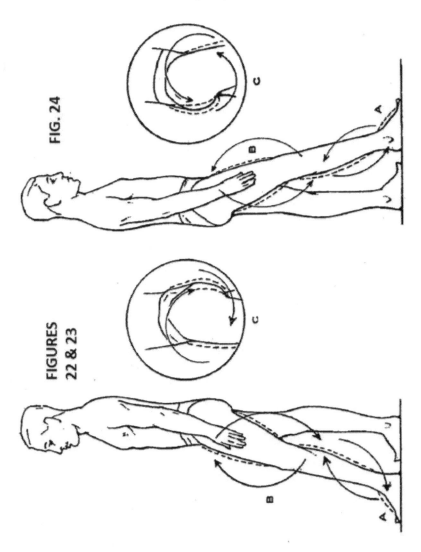

FIGURES 25 AND 26

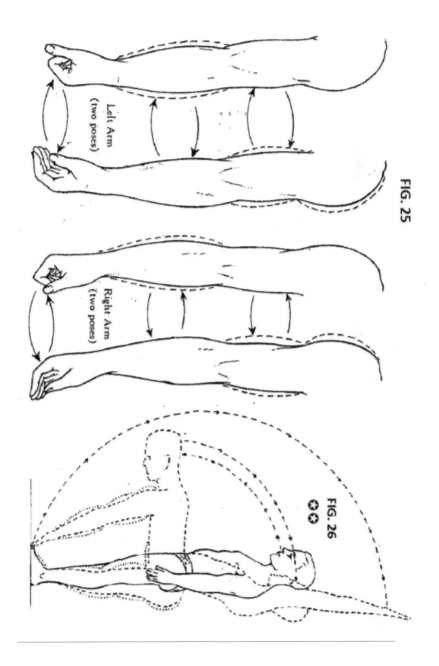

Left Arm
(two poses)

FIG. 25

Right Arm
(two poses)

FIG. 26

Fig. 25

1. Tense HIGH left forearm with Will, fist closed.
2. Relax and immediately tense HIGH left upper arm, fist open. keeping the lower left arm at right angles to the upper, slightly pressing the upper against side.
3. Relax.

Repeat, alternating thrice.

Repeat same exercise with right forearm and right upper arm, alternating thrice.

 Fig. 26

1. Stand erect.
2. Bend forward.
3. Keep .knee straight.
4. Try to touch feet with bands, slowly exhaling* and relaxing all body parts.
5. Slowly raise body and arms along with the head, inhaling* *slowly* to the full extent and tensing HIGH all body parts with Will from "down up"
6. Bend body backward slightly.
7. Again bend body forward and slowly exhale, trying to touch feet and relaxing body parts "up down."
   Repeat thrice or more.
8. Relax arms and stand erect.
   * **See Instruction 13, Page 3** [current document P. 7 and above]

[Original Pamphlet p. 13]

FIGURES 27 AND 28

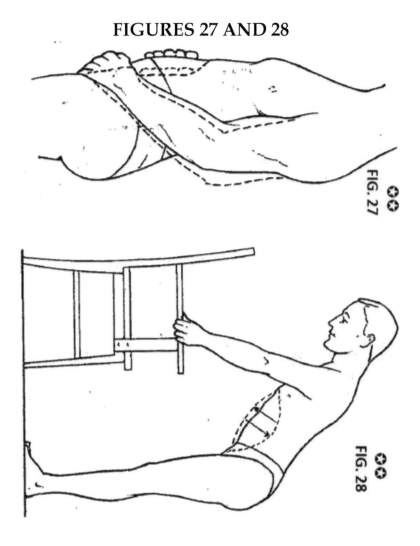

FIG. 27

FIG. 28

LESSON THREE -- PART I

"Tense with will; Relax and feel."*

EXERCISES of SPECIAL PARTS

Stomach Exercises, Helping Peristaltic Movement and Digestion, Eliminating Constipation, and Reducing Obesity.

✪✪Fig. 27.

Stand erect.

Close eyes.

Press both hands on abdomen, one above the other.

Contract and tense HIGH lower portion. See (*a*) in **Fig. 27**.

Hold while; contracting and tensing HIGH upper portion. See (*b*) in **Fig. 27**.

Relax both.

Repeat Eight Times.

✪✪Fig. 28

Stoop forward grasping arms of chair.

Hold arms straight.

Exhale completely.

With breath thus expelled slowly cave in abdomen AS FAR AS POSSIBLE, then push it out as far as possible.

Repeat alternately (with breath still expelled) four or more times. Then inhale.

Repeat exercise at least five times. ■

EXERCISE FOR WAIST.

✪ Fig. 29

This frees the thorax and promotes flexibility of movement, so essential in dancing and other artistic exercises. It is conducive to slimness and strength of waist.

Stand erect, feet apart.

Relax.

Tense HIGH and hold left foot, right foot, left calf, right calf, left thigh, right thigh, left haunch and right haunch.

Hold firm and straight from hips down.

---

* Remember this motto all through the exercises.

28

■ VERY IMPORTANT: When you have mastered this you will be able, by and by, taking the same position as in **Fig. 28**, to make, with your breath expelled, a WAVY MOVEMENT of the bands of vertical muscles running over the abdomen. Ordinarily do it eight times. Its effect is marvelous. See Page 5, **(c)** and **(d)** for details. [current document P. 9 and above]

[Original Pamphlet p. 14]

FIGURES 29 AND 32

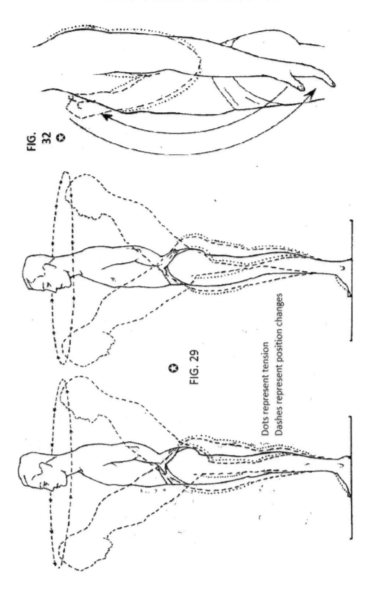

FIGURES 30 AND 31

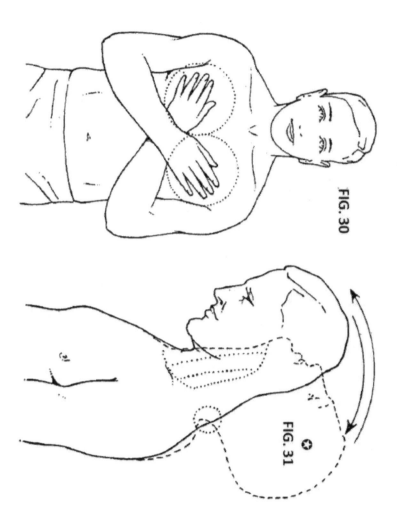

FIG. 30

FIG. 31

FIGURES 33, 34 AND 35

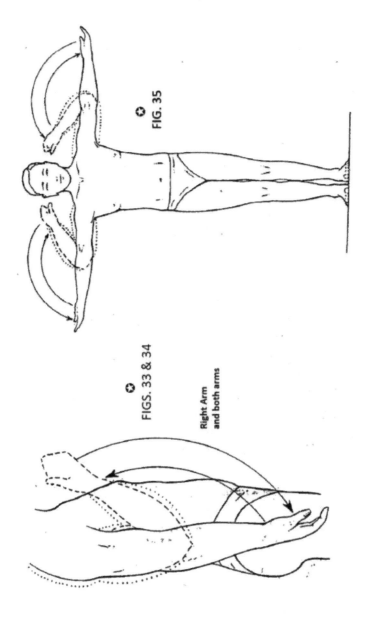

5. Relax upper part of body.
6. Bend forward at the waist as far as possible,
7. Rotate thrice upper part from front to left, back, right, front again, making a *perfectly* horizontal circle with the head. The position of the legs will of course follow the movement of the upper part of the body.
   Reverse and Rotate Thrice. Relax.

EXERCISE FOR THE CHEST.
Fig. 30

1. Stand erect.
2. Press left hand of right chest and right hand on left chest.
3. Slowly tense HIGH both chest and muscles.
4. Relax.
   Repeat Process Three Time or More.

EXERCISE FOR THROAT

 EXERCISE FOR THROAT. **Fig. 31**

Increases circulation in the brain, also memory and mental efficiency, and helps adjustment of the upper vertebrae.
1. Tensing throat muscles HIGH, throw head backwards.
2. Relax and throw head forward, chin falling on chest — with sharp downward snap so that a pull is felt on the upper vertebrae.
   Repeat Five Times or More.

[Original Pamphlet p. 15]

FIGURES 36 AND 37(a)

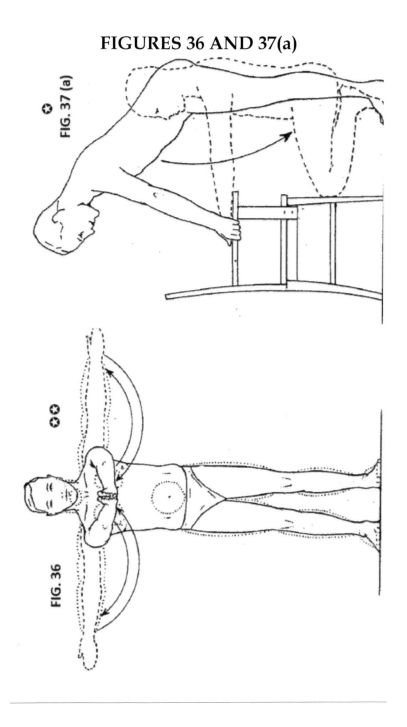

FIGURES 37(b) AND 38

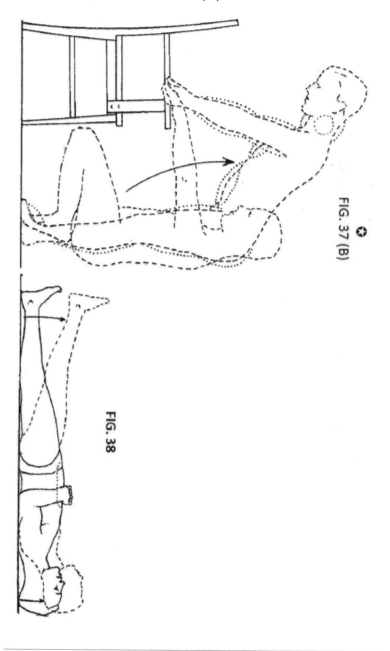

FIG. 37 (B)

FIG. 38

FIGURES 39 AND 40

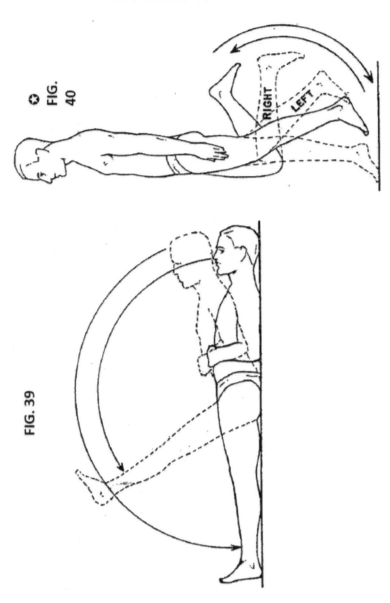

LESSON THREE -- PART II

"Tense with will; Relax and feel"*

⭐ (A) FIG. 32

1. Stand erect.
2. Relax arms hanging loosely at sides.
3. Palms open front.
4. Tense simultaneously LEFT HAND, LEFT FOREARM and UPPER ARM.
5. Slowly, with MAXIMUM tension, raise the forearm as high as possible, closing fists and feeling as though lifting a very heavy weight, and *vibrating* arms as they go up.
6. All the time keep upper left arm at side,
   Relax and drop left forearm.
   Repeal Thrice.

The same Exercise with right arm, **Fig. 33,** repeating thrice.

Take the same exercise with both arms together, FIG. **34.** ⭐

⭐ Exercise (B) FIG. **35**

1. Stretch arms at right angles to the spine.
2. Palms up.
3. Tense arms HIGH simultaneously.
4. Bend with HIGH tension at elbow, as if pulling weights, until hands reach shoulders, closing fists as they near shoulders and *vibrating* arms as they fold.
5. Relax, holding position. (**Fig. 35** does not show this.)
6. Tense again and extend arms slowly to the position from which they started.
7. Relax holding position.
   Repeat Thrice or More.
   Relax and drop hands.

 EXERCISE (C) **Fig. 36**

(To strengthen lungs and even circulation)
1. Stand erect, extend arms at right angles to the spine.
2. Open palms.
3. Slowly exhale■ bringing palms together in front.

*Remember this motto all through the exercises.
■ **See Instruction 13, Page 3.** [current document P. 7 and above]
[Original Pamphlet p. 16]

4.   Slowly inhale,* tensing all body parts HIGH from "down up" and extending arms with clenched fists to the first position.

5.   Slowly relax all body parts from "up down" and exhale,* slowly bringing palms together in front.

Repeat at Least Three Times.

Relax and Drop Arms.

⭐ EXERCISE (D) FIG. 37 **(A)**   FIG. 37 **(B)**

1.   See **Fig. 37 (a)** Grasp arms of a chair bending forward.
2.   Feet apart.
3.   *Exhale** and quickly relax to a sitting position on heels.
4.   See **Fig. 37 (*b*)**. Inhale,* slowly tensing HIGH all body parts "down up," 1 to 20 while rising to first position.
5.   Relax

Repeat Thrice

Return to standing position.

NOTE: Do this exercise 10 to 25 times, increasing gradually, disregarding tension or breathing. This strengthens hip, thigh muscles, and joints.

EXERCISE (E) **FIG. 38**

(To adjust the spine and reduce obesity)

1.   Lie down on back.
2.   Clasp hands on abdomen.
3.   Lift head and feet together, balancing body on hips.
4.   Holding breath, mentally count 1 to 6.
5.   Relax, and drop feet and head.

Duration is according to individual rapacity.

Repeat Twice

Exercise (F) **FIG. 39**

1.   Take same position.
2.   Rock back and forth several times, like a seesaw.

Do not do this until Exercise (E) is mastered.

⭐ (G) **FIG. 40** (RUNNING WHILE IN POSITION)

1.   Stand erect.
2.   Rapidly jump upland down, touching the floor alternately with LEFT and RIGHT foot while you kick the backs of thighs alternately with RIGHT and LEFT calf.

At Least Half a Minute

* **See Instructions 13, Page 3.** [current document P. 7 and above]
Never forget the paramount importance of the application of maximum
Will Power every time you induce tension in the above exercises.

[Original Pamphlet p. 17]

HIGHEST TECHNIQUE OF CONCENTRATION
LESSON IV

CONSCIOUS BREATHLESSNESS IS DEATHLESSNESS

Breath is life. If you can do without breath you can control life, prolong it and rise above it — to Soul, while living. In order to be without breath you cannot start by forcing or suppressing it the lungs — you have to watch it. This is the preliminary method.

You can practice this lesson any time. Sit erect wherever you are with a little forward chest and relax. Close your eyes (or direct both of your half-opened eyes toward the center of the eyebrows). With the GREATEST CALMNESS feel your breath NATURALLY going in and coming out. As it goes in move the index finger of your right hand toward the thumb and mentally chant (without moving your tongue) "Hong." As it goes out move the index finger away from the thumb and mentally chant "Saw." Do not IN ANY WAY USE MENTAL WILLINGNESS or FORCE to let the breath in or out. While practicing this have the calm attitude that you are a SILENT OBSERVER of your natural breath coming in and going out, of which you are not generally conscious. The movement of the index finger is only to differentiate inhalation from exhalation. With the greatest reverence and attention practice this at least ten minutes each time after the fifth lesson. The longer, the better. You can do it at leisure time (during day or night). You will feel the greatest calmness in you and by and by realize yourself as Soul, superior to and existing independently of this material body. "Hong" means Soul. "Saw" means The Great Spirit.

Always sit on a straight chair with a woolen blanket placed over it and running down under the feet. Face the East and sit erect without touching the back of the chair with your back. You ought to practice this method during your leisure periods, too, when you are on the bus or the trolley car or sitting anywhere doing nothing. Just watch the breath and mentally chant "Hong," "Saw" without moving the finger or closing the eyes or directing them toward the centre of the eyebrows, which might attract attention of people around you. Just keep your eyes open without winking, looking straight ahead at some specific point.

"I die daily." I Cor.1:31: Rev. 2:10, 11;9: 6; 14: 13; John II: 23-26

HIGHEST TECHNIQUE OF CONCENTRATION

LESSON V

CONSCIOUS CONTACT WITH COSMIC CONSCIOUSNESS.
=========

"In the beginning was the word, the word was with God, the word was God." (John I:I)

Every place has its distinctive influence on the mind. A kitchen produces the consciousness of food, cooking or eating, a parlor that of chatting, and a library that of reading. So you must make up your mind to get a suitable place for practicing concentration. The moment you go there let spiritual, introspective or silence consciousness surround you. Have a little temple or church in your home. At least fix up a closet or small room -- not too cold nor too warm – solely for this purpose. Place an arm-chair there. Put a woolen blanket on the chair running partly down on the floor. Sit it erect in the chair facing east with your feet on the blanket. Make the room dark or dimly lighted, if you like. Pray to the Great Spirit with a reverential attitude, "O Great Spirit, help me to gather my inner powers and realize Thee through vibrations. The universe is projected from Thee through Cosmic Vibration, it is sustained by Thee through Cosmic Vibration. The Vibration pervades everywhere. Thou art transcendentally Omnipresent in the Vibration. Through vibrations in me help me to realize Thee inwardly and outwardly. Awaken my sleeping powers. Rouse my infinite energy. Lead me on to the vision of The Glorious Light. Peace."

Then place two pillows on the arms of the chair, rest your elbows on them. With the thumb of each hand press the little cartilage of the external ear (at the back end of the cheek bone) against each ear-hole, shutting out all outward sounds and noises. Close eyes. Place the tip of the little finger of each hand at the end of each eye-ball over the eye-lid. Press the eye-balls very gently that they do not roll or wiggle. Rest other fingers of both the hands on the forehead. With closed eyebrows CONVERGE your gaze to the central point in front of you towards the junction of the eyebrows, and keep it fixed. You may feel a little ache at the beginning, but practice will make this easy. This will improve your eyesight. By practice you will see there the astral electronic light -- a "white luminous sun," a dark round spot inside it and a star inside it the dark spot. This is the Third Eye — the Door. (St. John 10:9.) "If therefore thine eye be single, thy whole body shall be full of light." Matthew 6:22. That is, if you see the Third Eye and be in it, you will feel and know by and by, the astral or electronic body, corresponding to your physical body. Many other lights of different shapes and hues, stars, etc., will come, but do not be satisfied until you get the above one. With your eyes fixed in this position (or in the astral light that will come through practice) MENTALLY chant "OM" "OM" (making no sound, nor whisper nor movement of the tongue). KEEP ON LISTENING IN THE INSIDE OF THE RIGHT EAR to any vibration you hear. Be ONE with the vibration with reverence. (a) You may hear inside the ear different physical vibrations of heart beat, lungs, or diaphragm movement, circulation, etc. Go deeper. (b) As you listen on your concentration will deepen of itself and you will begin to hear the astral vibrations − the vibrations of your electronic body − cricket sound, bumble-bee, flute, harp, distant gong etc., or the ocean roar. (Revelation 1:15). (c) Then by gradual practice you will hear the Symphony of Rolling Om (the vibration of your spiritual or causal body), filling your body and mind. Read or chant the poem on "OM" in our book "Songs of the Soul." You must get beyond the stage of hearing what is ordinarily known as "ringing in the ears" to get to the higher vibrations.

Hear any vibration, that at first comes to you, with the greatest intensity of mental effort and be one with it. Immerse your mind in it. All the other vibrations will come to you, by and by, through practice. Put forth all your active mental effort in hearing the vibrations. Let the chanting of "OM" and keeping the eyes in position be done automatically − without mental effort. Afterwards when you are through with listening, put forth active mental effort to see the "luminous sun," once or twice. By practice you will be able to see the "sun" always while hearing the vibrations with closed ears.

Practice this for 10 to 15 minutes in the morning, 20 to 30 minutes or more before going to bed. Bow to God when you are through with practicing. Both intensity of mental effort while practicing and duration of practice are needed to reach higher and higher states of concentration.

You have absolutely no idea of the effects this technique will produce. If you practice it regularly, faithfully and reverentially you will feel them all, by and by. With open ears you will be able to hear the vibration at any time, especially at night and will be in time intuitionally in tune with the Cosmic Vibration (or Rolling OM). This Cosmic Vibration is not only inside you but everywhere in the universe. All realizations can not be named here.

Concentration Lessons will open the door to inspiration and definite intuitions of all sorts, not named here.

They will produce an urge in you towards the attainment of Higher Spiritual Consciousness. Not only that, they will create the capacity to switch over quickly from one plane of feeling, thought or realization to its* corresponding higher plane.

Remember the practice of the technique will give you a great command over your mind. It will enable you to focus your mind quickly in the most intense way on any object of thought — physical, intellectual or spiritual. This is as true as the sun's rising in the east. It will also produce in you tremendous power of doing active works in life. Above all, it will bring you in touch with the Super-conscious (the soud and the Great Spirit), giving you wonderful peace, harmony and poise of mind so essential to the higher living of life.

It soothes and rests the nerves and brings about the most desirable bodily conditions.

OM -- Word -- Amen -- means the Cosmic Vibration, emanating from the Great Spirit, the beginning of Creation (John 1:1, Rev. 3:14).

For personal use only by the one who enrolls for the lessons, unless privilege to the contrary is given.

FURTHER HINTS AS TO THE CONCENTRATION LESSONS

If time allows, practice the concentration lessons longer than said before. Aside from inward experiences as written there, they produce the greatest calmness. Hold to that **calm effect** of the concentration lessons **during and immediately after** the practice as long as it is possible for you. Apply that calmness in practical situations of life — in dealings with people, in studying, in business, if you like, in thinking, in controlling yourself, if control is thought necessary, in getting rid of any fixed mental or physiological habit or condition that is considered unnecessary or harmful, and so forth. Whenever situations demand recall immediately in mind the calmness felt during and after concentration and fall right into that state, and meet situations from that calm centre. Remember while practicing concentration deep intensity of mind is necessary, but that does not mean that there should be any **strain** or **strenuousness** present. Practice it with reverence, and feel that in calmness and in listening to the vibrations, you are contacting the Great Spirit who is present within you as soul and whose expression is vibration. Results you will positively feel. Calmnesss you will most certainly have. But the highest intuitions come after a prolonged practice. Further, this technique puts you, by and by, in touch with the unexplored reservoir of power. Do not be impatient. Keep on. Get it into your regular routine. **Most beneficial effect flows silently over the whole mental and physiological constitution**, though often unnoticed. Highest results, as in everything else, cannot be got in one day. Practice, practice, practice and apply. We are talking from experience.

Other books authored or edited by Castellano-Hoyt

Phineas F. Bresee: A Prince in Israel: A Biography,
by Rev. E.A. Girvin
ISBN-13: 978-1506117997, ISBN-10: 1506117996, BISAC:
Biography & Autobiography / Religious.
Rev. E.A. Girvin's biography of Dr. Bresee was a monumental undertaking and is an outstanding success. He details the historical and theological issues facing Dr. Bresee and the host of second blessing holiness leaders in America as they formed the Church of the Nazarene.

Bud Robinson Stories and Sketch, Rev. C.T. Corbett
ISBN-13: 978-1505723526; ISBN-10: 1505723523
BISAC: Religion / Inspirational
These stories give a fresh look into the spirit of a spiritual giant. Especially refreshing and startling is Uncle Bud's description of his sanctification experience out in the corn fields!

My Hospital Experience,
Rev. Bud Robinson,
ISBN-13: 978-1505658279; ISBN-10: 1505658276
BISAC: Religion / Inspirational
Evangelist Uncle Bud Robinson's hospital experience is the first Western description of "going to heaven," communing with the saints, the angels, and Lord Jesus. He is one of the first Christian ministers to realize that heaven is for real and that it is our real home.

YOGODA or Tissue-Will System of Physical Perfection,
Yogananda
[This is a reprint of Swami Yogananda's 1925 course on energization and will power. This is historical. Nothing medical nor scientific is implied or endorsed by the editor in distributing this

information. The value of Swamiji's insight is incalculable and the editor is happy to be distributing this pamphlet to a world-wide audience. Jai, guru!]

Yogiraj Shri Shri Lahiri Mahasaya,
Jogesh Bhattacharya
This is a reprint of Prof. Jogesh Bhattacharya's biography of His Holiness Sri Sri Lahiri Mahasaya. Professor undertook the effort at the behest of his guru Sri Sri Anilanandaji. The editor is happy to make this important book available once again to a world wide audience.

Scientific Healing Affirmations: 2014 Reprint of the 1925 2nd edition,
Yogananda
2014 reprint of Swami Yogananda's 1925 second edition of this famous treatise on mental and physiological techniques for healing in body, mind and soul.

Descriptive Outline of YOGODA: Reprint of 1930 11th edition,
Yogananda and Nerode
Historic statement of the meaning of Yogananda's teachings. The booklet itself is important for those who are interested in the history of the movement that culminated in the formation of the organization "Self-Realization Fellowship."

Stories of Mukunda,
Donald K. Walters, Swami Kriyananda
[As a Christmas present to the younger monks at
Self-Realization Fellowship headquarters Minister
Kriyananda compiled these 14 loving
reminiscences of their guru's early childhood. The
book has been abandoned long by both SRF
Publishers and by Ananda Publishers. The editor
is happy to make this edition available once again
to a world-wide audience.]

Reincarnation,
Ranendra Kumar Das
The concept of reincarnation is endorsed in almost
all the major religions of the world, including the
Christian. Sri Das goes into historic and scriptural
detail regarding the meaning and helpfulness of
this timeless teaching.

It Can Be Done,
Ranendra Kumar Das
A close disciple of Paramhansa Yogananda,
kriyaban minister Sri Das surveys the timeless
principles for successful material and spiritual
living.

Made in the USA
Middletown, DE
05 October 2015